It's About Time

Jack Beers

The small hand
on a clock is called
the hour hand.
The hour hand
is pointing to the 7.
It means the time is
about seven o'clock.

Kelly
wakes up.

Casey wakes up.

The big hand
on a clock is called
the minute hand.
It is pointing
straight up.
It means the time is
exactly seven o'clock.

The hour hand is
between the 7
and the 8.
It is halfway between
the 7 and the 8.
It means the time is
about half past seven.

Casey and Kelly
eat breakfast.

The minute hand points straight down. It means that the time is exactly half past seven.

The hour hand
is pointing
close to the 9.
It points
just before the 9.
It means the time
is just before
nine o'clock.

Casey and Kelly say
goodbye to Mom.

Casey watches Kelly
go to her classroom.

The hour hand
is pointing
close to the 9.
It points
just past the 9.
It means the time
is just past
nine o'clock.

The hour hand is
pointing halfway
between the 9
and the 10.
What time
is it now?

Casey's class listens
to Ms. Chin read
from a book.

The minute hand is pointing straight down. What time is it now?

Casey and
her class
enjoy recess.

Casey and Kelly eat together.

Lunch starts at twelve o'clock.

Is it lunch time yet?

How can you tell?

Casey is in math class.

Is it half past twelve?
Or is it half past one?

Casey's favorite class is Chinese.

Chinese class starts
at one o'clock.
Has class started yet?

Kelly is practicing for a play.

School ends at 3:00.
Is it time to go home yet?

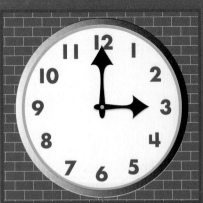

Goodbye, Casey.
Goodbye, Kelly.

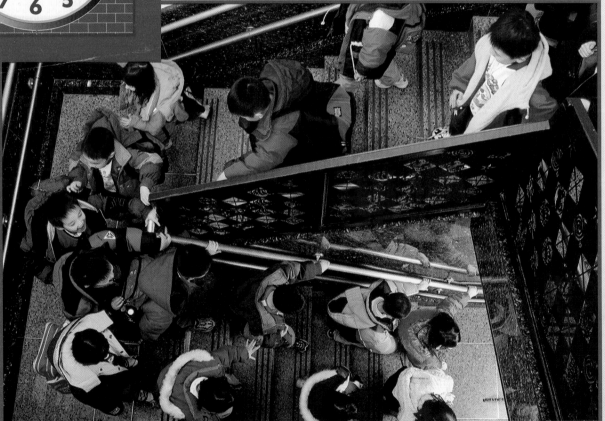